Horribly Awful DAD JOKES

 PETER PAUPER PRESS, INC.
Rye Brook, New York

PETER PAUPER PRESS

In 1928, at the age of twenty-two, Peter Beilenson began printing books on a small press in the basement of his parents' home in Larchmont, New York. Peter—and later, his wife, Edna—sought to create fine books that sold at "prices even a pauper could afford."

Today, still family owned and operated, Peter Pauper Press continues to honor our founders' legacy of quality, value, and fun for big kids and small kids alike.

Designed by Heather Zschock
Images used under license from Shutterstock.com

Copyright © 2023
Peter Pauper Press, Inc.
3 International Drive
Rye Brook, NY 10573 USA

Published in the United Kingdom and Europe by
Peter Pauper Press, Inc. c/o White Pebble International
Units 2-3, Spring Business Park
Stanbridge Road
Havant, Hampshire PO9 2GJ, UK

Visit us at www.peterpauper.com

Contents

CONGRATS ON BEING YOU
(a dad, that is)

Hey Dad,

Let's face it. There's no one quite like you. And you deserve something special to go with that "#1 Dad" mug you *totally* love.

Say hello to **HORRIBLY AWFUL DAD JOKES**. This book features the best of the worst! Whether you're looking to wisecrack with friends about work, engage in some tried-and-true toilet humor, or make your kid beg for mercy with the ten millionth knock-knock joke, we've got you covered. You can even poke fun at parenting itself with some jokes about the joys (and horrors) of raising a family.

They say laughter is the most beautiful music, but people who say that haven't heard the sound of your family groaning as you open this book to a fresh page. And because we're so generous, we've also included a section at the end full of perfect comebacks to some common sayings, requests, and complaints.

Now thank your kid for this gift and make them live to regret it!

Technology

Need some high-tech laughs? If you're restarting the router, suffering through a power outage, or waiting in line for the newest smartphone, distract your family with these state-of-the-art jokes.

**What does a baby computer
call its father?**
Data.

**Why couldn't the computer buy
a new sweater?**
It spent all its cache.

**What do you call an iPhone with
no sense of humor?**
Overly Siri-ous.

What do you call it when an
IT person gets hand surgery?
Tech knuckle support.

What's the most common lie?
*"I have read and agreed to the
terms and conditions."*

**What happens when a hard drive
gets into a fight?**
It asks for backup.

Why was the smartphone taking blurry photos?
It lost all of its contacts.

What's a computer's favorite snack?
Microchips.

Why should you never use "beef stew" as a password?
It's not stroganoff.

Why did the PowerPoint presentation cross the road?
To get to the other slide.

Why was the laptop late to class?
It had a hard drive.

What should you do if your Nintendo game ends in a tie?
Ask for a Wii-match.

What do you get when you cross a dog with a computer?
A machine with a bark worse than its byte.

Did you hear about the cell phone wedding?
*The ceremony was fine, but the
reception was amazing.*

Why do cell phones ring?
Because they can't knock.

**How many programmers does it take
to change a light bulb?**
None, it's a hardware problem.

Which computer has the best voice?
A Dell.

**Why should you put airbags
on a computer?**
In case it crashes.

What do you call a computer superhero?
A screen saver.

Why did the cat sit on the computer?
To keep an eye on the mouse.

**How are conspiracy theories like
moon landings?**
They're all fake.

Why did the computer catch a cold?
Someone left its Windows open.

**Why did the cell phone go
to the dentist?**
To get its Bluetooth checked.

**What does a proud computer dad
call his kid?**
A microchip off the old block.

How do trees use the internet?
They just log in.

**What do you call two monkeys
sharing an Amazon account?**
Prime mates.

**Did you know there are 10 types
of people in the world?**
*Those who understand binary,
and those who don't.*

Why was the computer drunk?
It took too many screenshots.

What do you call having your grandmother on speed dial?
Instagram.

You know who my worst enema is?
Autocorrect.

What did the cat say on the conference call?
Can you hear me meow?

Why was the computer so angry?
It had a chip on its shoulder.

Why did the computer get glasses?
To improve its web-sight.

Why did the computer sneeze?
It caught a virus.

Where do computers go dancing?
The disk-o.
But that's not the only music they like.
They also appreciate tech-no.

**How did the computer prepare
for a day at the beach?**
It surfed the net.

**What type of computer would
a horse like to eat?**
A Macintosh.

**Two hackers are trapped on a rowboat.
What do they do?**
Start phishing.

What's a computer's favorite animal?
A RAM.

**What do you get if you cross an
elephant with a computer?**
Lots of memory.

Sports

Whether you're at your kid's soccer game, watching football, or playing golf, we've got jokes for any arena. Perfect for moments that require a quick recovery.

**Why does a pitcher raise one leg
when he throws the ball?**
If he raised them both, he'd fall down.

**What's the difference between a thief
and an umpire?**
*One steals watches and the other watches
steals.*

**Where do they keep the largest
diamond in New York City?**
Yankee Stadium.

**What do you call a football player with
long legs who builds houses?**
A car-punter.

Why did the soccer ball quit the team?
It was tired of being kicked around.

Did you hear the joke about the pop fly?
Forget it. It's way over your head.

**What do you call a person who walks
back and forth screaming one minute and
then sits down to start crying the next?**
A football coach.

Why was the basketball player sitting on the sidelines drawing chickens?

The coach wanted her to learn how to draw fouls.

Why do Canadians always beat Germans in hockey?

Canadians bring their "eh" game. The Germans bring their wurst.

What are the rules for zebra baseball?

Three stripes and you're out.

Why is tennis such a loud sport?

The players raise a racket.

Why do hockey rinks have rounded edges?

If they were 90 degrees, the ice would melt.

Why did the football coach go to the bank?

To get his quarter back.

Where does a hockey player's salary come from?

The tooth fairy.

Why can't basketball players go on vacation?

They're not allowed to travel.

I couldn't remember how to throw a boomerang.
But eventually it came back to me.

What has eighteen legs and catches flies?
A baseball team.

What's the difference between hockey and professional wrestling?
In hockey, the fights are real.

Which football player wears the biggest helmet?
The one with the biggest head.

Which goalie can jump higher than the crossbars?
All of them. Crossbars can't jump.

Why do baseball games happen at night?
The bats sleep during the day.

How do football players deal with their problems?
They tackle them head-on.

**The boating store in town had
a big sale on canoes.**
It was quite an oar deal.

**What's the difference between
a Yankees fan and a dentist?**
*One roots for the Yanks, and the
other yanks for the roots.*

**What does a basketball player do
once he loses his sight?**
Become a referee.

**What do you get when you cross a
running back with the Invisible Man?**
Scoring like no one has ever seen.

**Why can't all-star football
players listen to music?**
They break all the records.

**What do you get when you cross
a quarterback with a carpet?**
A throw rug.

**Where do football teams go when they
need replacement uniforms?**
New Jersey.

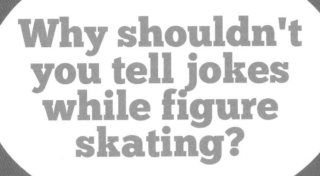

**How did Americans steal the name
for football?**

They grabbed it and ran.

Why don't grasshoppers watch soccer?

They prefer cricket.

**What do hockey players and magicians
have in common?**

They both do hat tricks.

**Hockey players are known for
their summer teeth.**

Summer here, summer there.

**Why are soccer players
so good at math?**

They know how to use their heads.

**Did you hear about the referee who
got fired from the NBA?**

Apparently, he was a whistleblower.

I watched hockey before it was cool.

It was swimming. I watched swimming.

**What can you use to light
up a stadium?**

A soccer match.

**What do you call a boat full of
well-behaved golfers?**

Good sportsman-ship.

**Why should you never date
a tennis player?**

*Because love means nothing
to them.*

Pop Culture

Who needs late-night television when you've got jokes like these? Enjoy a chuckle during movie previews (but for the sake of the theater, and your poor family, please stop when the film starts).

What do you call it when Batman skips church?

Christian Bale.

How do celebrities stay cool?

They have so many fans.

What do you call security guards outside of a Samsung store?

Guardians of the Galaxy.

How does Reese eat cereal?

Witherspoon.

Why did the Jedi cross the road?

To get to the dark side.

What did Obi-Wan say to Luke at the breakfast table?

"Use the fork, Luke."

Why did Adele cross the road?

To say hello from the other side.

What's a cow's favorite sci-fi TV show?

Dr. Moo.

What did Simba say when the zebra wanted to switch roles for the day?

"Okay, I'm game."

I wasn't sure Netflix would be successful.

Then again, Stranger Things have happened.

What do you call a fight between celebrities?

Star Wars!

What's in Squidward's underwear?

Squid marks.

How do Wookiees like their cookies?

Chewie.

What's the difference between Spider-Man and Superman?

Peter Parker can shoot webs. Clark Kent.

What did Elvis say after he was bitten by a vampire?

"Fang you. Fang you very much."

How did Elsa lose her balloon?

She let it go.

What do you call a deep-sea Transformer?

Octopus Prime.

What do you call a big fish that makes you an offer you can't refuse?

The Codfather.

Why couldn't Dorothy tell the bad witch from the good witch?

Because she couldn't tell which was witch!

Why do you tell actors to break a leg?

Because every film has a cast.

Where did Lassie become a star?

Collie-wood.

A woman went to the doctor and said, "Please help me! Every time I stand up quickly, I see Mickey Mouse, Goofy, and Donald Duck."

The doctor replied, "I see. And how long have you been getting these Disney spells?"

**My friend said I'm annoying because
I relate everything to Batman.**
She's such a Joker!

**Why couldn't Princess Leia
find love?**
She was looking in Alderaan places.

**What did Thor, Iron Man, and the Hulk
say when they went into IKEA?**
"Avengers, assemble!"

**Did you hear about the Scooby-Doo
villain who almost became a world
champion goat herder?**
*He would have won, if it weren't for
all those modaling kids.*

Why do rabbits like action movies?
Because they're hare-raising.

**What does Kermit say when
eating dinner?**
"Time's fun when you're having flies."

What did Yoda say when he saw himself on TV?

"HDMI."

What's the difference between Iron Man and Aluminum Man?

Iron Man defeats villains, but Aluminum Man just foils their plans.

Why won't Mr. Krabs give to charity?

He's a shellfish penny pincher.

How come U2 still haven't found what they're looking for?

Because the streets have no names.

What's a blue whale's favorite James Bond film?

License to Krill.

What's a dentist's favorite movie?

Plaque to the Future.

Why was Aunt May worried about Spider-Man?

He was spending too much time on the web.

How do Jedi say goodbye?
"See you Leia."

Did you hear about the Minecraft movie?
It's a blockbuster.

**What was the most popular kids' movie
in Ancient Greece?**
Troy Story.

**Why did King Kong climb the
Empire State Building?**
He couldn't fit in the elevator.

**How do you watch movies inside
a haunted house?**
On a wide-scream TV.

What does Calvin feed Hobbes?
Nothing, he's already stuffed.

**What do you call a gingerbread man
with one leg bitten off?**
Limp Bizkit.

**Why did Tarzan spend so much time
on the golf course?**
He was perfecting his swing.

Where do mermaids see movies?

At the dive-in.

**What does Homer Simpson
use to make bread?**
D'oh!

**How did Darth Vader know what Luke
got him for Christmas?**
He felt his presents.

What is Forrest Gump's email password?
1Forrest1.

Who was Tolkien's favorite rock star?
Elvish Presley.

**Rick Astley will give you any movie
from his collection except one.**
He's never gonna give you Up.

**My friend said she wouldn't talk to me
because of my obsession with the Monkees.
I thought she was joking.**
But then I saw her face.

Two Beach Boys walk into a bar.
"Round?"
"Round."
"Get a round?"
"I'll get a round!"

Why did Bono fall off the stage?

He was too close to The Edge.

**How do you turn a duck into
a soul singer?**

Put it in the microwave until its Bill Withers.

**What do you call two synth musicians
running an animal rescue?**

Pet Shop Boys.

**What do the movies *The Sixth Sense*
and *Titanic* have in common?**

Icy dead people.

What's E.T. short for?

He's got little legs.

**What did the Tin Man say when he
got run over by a steamroller?**

"Curses! Foil again."

Science

What happens when you mix hydrogen, oxygen, and a dad joke? Your kid laughs and spurts water all over the place. Or your kid continues to drink while rolling their eyes. A successful experiment either way!

**Did you hear about the book I'm
reading on antigravity?**
It's impossible to put down.

**What do you call Iron Man and the
Silver Surfer working together?**
Alloys.

**What type of fish is made of two
sodium atoms?**
Two Na.

**What do you call a scientist's
accountant?**
A buy-ologist.

**How did the chemist feel about oxygen
and potassium hanging out?**
OK.

**What did one atom say
to the other?**
I've got my ion you.

**How much room does fungi
need to grow?**

As mushroom as possible.

Why are skeletons so calm?

Because nothing gets under their skin.

**What's brown and sounds
like a bell?**

Dung.

**What did the photon say when asked
if it needed to check a bag?**

"No thanks, I'm traveling light."

How do you organize a space party?

You planet.

**How do you identify a
dogwood tree?**

You check its bark.

**What did the biologist wear
to impress their date?**

Designer genes.

Why are chemists so good at fixing problems?
They have all the solutions.

What did the dung beetle say when it walked into a bar?
"Excuse me, is this stool taken?"

What kind of music do planets listen to?
Nep-tunes.

Did you know milk is the fastest liquid on Earth?
It's pasteurize before you even see it.

Which is faster, hot or cold?
Hot—you can catch a cold.

Why are there only bad science jokes left?
Because all the good ones argon.

Why is electricity such a great student?
It conducts itself well.

Why did the chicken cross the Möbius strip?
To get to the same side.

Schrödinger's cat walks into a bar...
And doesn't.

**What did one tectonic plate say
when it bumped into the other?**
Sorry! My fault.

Why shouldn't you trust atoms?
They make up everything.

**Why does no one talk to
pi at parties?**
It goes on forever.

What's a chemist's favorite pet?
A Laboratory Retriever.

**What did the cell say to its sister
when it stubbed its toe?**
Mitosis!

**How do scientists freshen
their breath?**
They use experi–mints.

**What does blood say when it's
trying to be optimistic?**
"B positive."

Did you know that all mushrooms are edible?
Well, some are only edible once.

**What did the thermometer tell
the graduated cylinder?**
*You may have graduated,
but I have more degrees.*

What do you do with a sick chemist?
*First you try helium, but if you can't
curium, you have to barium.*

**A neutron walked into a bar and said,
"How much for a beer?" What did
the bartender say?**
"For you, no charge."

**Three statisticians go hunting.
They spot a deer in the distance,
and the first one shoots about a foot
too high. The second one then takes
aim, but shoots about a foot too low.
What does the third one do?**
Yell, "We got it!"

**How should you reply to a text
telling you oxygen and magnesium
got together?**
OMg!

**Did you hear that scientists
finally discovered the gene
that causes shyness?**
*They would have found it earlier,
but it was hiding behind
two other genes.*

Why is ice such a hipster?
It was water before it got cool.

**Why couldn't the moon pay
for dinner?**
It was down to its last quarter.

**Do you know why they call me
DJ Enzyme?**
Because I'm always breaking it down.

**What's the difference between
a dog and a marine biologist?**
*One wags a tail and the other
tags a whale.*

**What do you call an acid with
a bad attitude?**
A-mean-oh acid.

Why do plants hate math?
It gives them square roots.

**Why does a burger have less
energy than a steak?**
A burger is in its ground state.

**What did the limestone say
to the geologist?**
"Don't take me for granite."

**Did you hear about the microbiologist
who traveled all over the world and
could speak ten languages?**
She was a woman of many cultures.

**How did the English major define
"microtome" on his biology exam?**
A very small book.

Why do chemists like nitrates?
They're cheaper than day rates.

Why did the biologist and physicist break up?

There was no chemistry.

Why did the amoeba cross the road?

It was time to split.

Did you know that you can hear the blood in your veins?

You just have to listen varicosely.

What part of the body lives longest?

Pupils. They dilate.

Why did the doctor take a red pen to work?

In case she needed to draw blood.

Toilet Humor

There's nothing as classic as this! It's the perfect literature to peruse on your porcelain throne.

Want to hear a poop joke?
Nah, they always stink.

**What did one piece of toilet paper
say to the other?**
"I'm feeling really wiped."

**Why didn't the toilet paper
cross the road?**
It got stuck in a crack.

**A little girl is walking along a country
road one day when she comes across a
farmer with a truck full of cow manure.
She asks him what he's going to do
with all that cow poop, and he tells
her that he's taking it home to
put on his strawberries.**
*She thinks for a moment and says,
"I don't know where you're from,
but where I'm from we put cream and
sugar on our strawberries."*

**Did you know that diarrhea
is hereditary?**
It runs in your jeans.

It's funny how corn maintains its shape after you poop it out.

And yet it tastes completely different.

What's the difference between bad and good toilet paper?

One is terrible, and the other is tearable.

Want to hear a Parent's Truth?

The farther you are from the bathroom, the more urgently your kid has to poop.

Did you hear about the constipated accountant?

He just couldn't budget.

One friend confesses to another, "I take a poop every morning at 8 a.m." The other replies, "Well, it's good to be regular. What's the problem?"

"I wake up at 9 a.m."

Why don't all banks have toilets?

Because not all banks accept deposits.

I had a bathroom emergency at work today.

It was so bad my coworker tried to open a window. We work on a submarine.

Why do ducks have feathers?

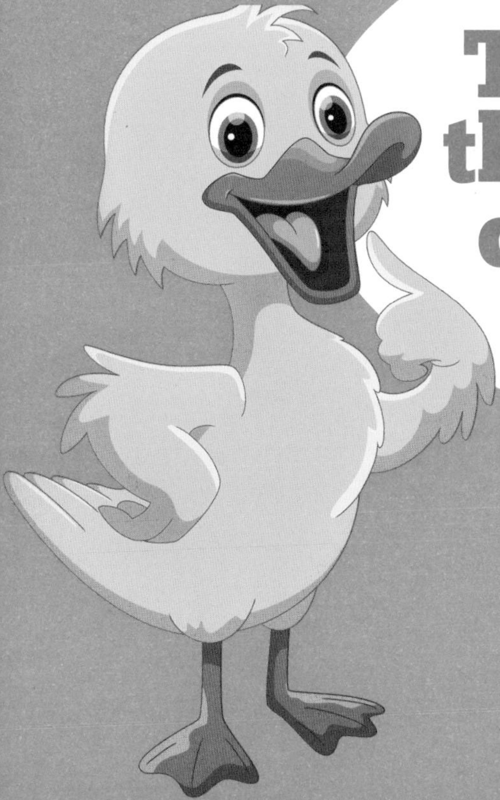

To cover their butt quacks.

What's brown and sticky?
A stick.

**What do you call the Queen
of England's farts?**
Noble gases.

**What kinds of poop jokes should
you never tell?**
The corny ones.

**If pooping is the call of nature,
what's farting?**
A missed call.

How is love like a fart?
*If you have to force it, it's
probably crap.*

**Did you hear about the constipated
mathematician?**
He worked it out with a pencil.

**Did you know that when you say
the word "poop," your mouth does the
same motion as your butthole?**
*The same is true for the phrase
"explosive diarrhea."*

Did you hear about the constipated composer?

He had problems with his last movement.

What's the definition of "surprise"?

A fart with a lump in it.

What's a surfer's second greatest fear?

A shart attack.

What's something you never appreciate until it's gone?

Toilet paper.

Do you know the difference between toilet paper and a shower curtain?

No? So you're the one!

Why did the chicken cross the road?

The chicken next to him farted.

What did Spock find in the Enterprise toilet?

The Captain's log.

What happened to the woman who ate four cans of alphabet soup?

She had a huge vowel movement.

How do you get the bathroom door unlocked?

You use a doo-key.

Living alone can sometimes be scary. But what can comfort you and freak you out at the same time?

A warm toilet seat.

Poop jokes aren't my favorite.

But I will admit they're number two.

Why did the toilet paper roll down the hill?

To get to the bottom.

Do you know why I love my toilet?

We've been through a lot of sh*t together.

What do you get when you cross a rhino and a toilet?

I don't know, but I'm not using that bathroom.

Did you hear about the movie *Constipated*?

It hasn't come out yet.

Did you hear about the movie *Diarrhea*?

It leaked, so they had to release it early.

Where do toilets come from?
They grow on toiletries.

How are children like farts?
You don't mind your own, but everyone else's are horrendous.

I tried explaining to my four-year-old daughter that it's perfectly normal to accidentally poop your pants.
But even now she's still making fun of me.

I like toilets for two reasons.
Number one and number two.

Doctors say that four out of five people suffer from diarrhea.
But doesn't that just mean ono guy likes it?

What do politicians and diapers have in common?
They both need to be changed often.

If you're American in the living room, what are you in the bathroom?
European.

**Why can't you hear a psychologist
in the bathroom?**
The "p" is silent.

**Last week, I ran out of toilet paper
and had to use newspaper instead.**
All I can say is that The Times
are really rough.

**The toilet paper shortages of the
Great Depression were as saddening
as they were illuminating.**
*They showed that when it comes down to it,
the average person really only cares
about their own behind.*

**What's the difference between
a toilet and a cemetery?**
*Nothing—when it's time to go,
it's time to go.*

**What's the quickest way to get in
touch with your inner self?**
Buy single-ply toilet paper.

**My roommate asked me to put
the toilet seat down.**
*So I ran into the bathroom and shouted,
"Nobody even likes you!"*

**Why did the Netherlands pass
a law making it illegal to flush
shoes down the toilet?**
There were too many clogs.

**What did the left eye say to
the right eye?**
*"Between you and me,
something smells."*

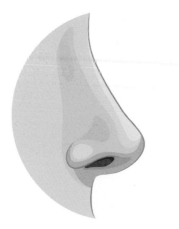

Hardly Working

When you can't bother your family, bother your coworkers! But for the sake of self-preservation, don't test these jokes out on your boss.

**Some people say the glass is half full,
and some say the glass is half empty.
What do engineers say?**

*They say the glass is twice as big
as necessary.*

Why is teamwork important?

It helps to be able to blame someone else.

**Some people learn from witnessing
the mistakes of others. How does
everyone else learn?**

Being the others.

**What do you call a plant that
manufactures okay products?**

A satis-factory.

What ruins a Friday?

When you realize it's actually Thursday.

**Who wins in a fight between
Sunday and Monday?**

Sunday. Monday is a weekday.

Do you know why people say I'm great at multitasking?
I can waste time, be unproductive, and procrastinate all at once.

What's another term for "résumé"?
A list of things I hope you never ask me to do.

What's the best way to use a stress ball?
Throw it at the last person to upset you.

How do you know when you've made it, professionally?
You have a desk where no one else can see your computer monitor.

What do you call exercise at the office?
Jumping to conclusions, pushing your luck, and dodging deadlines.

How do you define "discretion"?
Being able to raise your eyebrow instead of your voice.

**What should you do if at first
you don't succeed?**

Redefine success.

**What is a clean desk
a sign of?**

A cluttered desk drawer.

Why is a doctor always calm?

Because she has a lot of patients.

**Stealing ideas from one person is
called plagiarism. What do you
call stealing from many?**

Research.

**What did the employee do when the
boss said to have a good day?**

They went home.

**If every day is a gift, I'd like
a receipt for Monday.**

I want to exchange it for another Friday.

Why did the can crusher quit his job?

Because it was soda pressing.

**Whoever stole my copy of
Microsoft Office…**
I'll find you. You have my Word!

**Making mistakes proves you're human.
What does blaming your mistakes
on others prove?**
Management potential.

**Did I ever tell you I used to work
for a paper business?**
But then it folded.

**I also tried starting a hot air
balloon business…**
But it never took off.

**What's proof that the work week
is rough?**
*After Monday and Tuesday, even
the calendar says WTF.*

I don't mind coming to work…
*It's the eight–hour wait to go
home I can't stand.*

**How can you keep your
dreams alive?**

Hit the snooze button.

**There's a new trend in our office;
everyone is putting names
on their food.**

*I saw it today when I was eating
a sandwich named Stacy.*

What's an archaeologist?

Someone whose career is in ruins.

**Why did the scarecrow get
an award?**

Because it was outstanding its field.

**How do you determine the probability
of someone watching you?**

*It's always proportional to the stupidity
of what you're doing.*

What's a committee?

Twelve people doing the work of one.

Why was the taxi driver fired?
*Passengers didn't like it when
he went the extra mile.*

**What are the two types of people
who say very little?**
*Those who are quiet and those
who talk a lot.*

**What's the hardest thing
about business?**
Minding your own.

**What did the nearsighted optometrist
say when she was sick?**
"I can't see myself coming in today."

**What did the supervisor say
to the calendar?**
"Your days are numbered."

**What's the problem with
unemployment jokes?**
None of them work.

Why are construction workers great at parties?
They raise the roof.

Why do I drink coffee before work?
*I like to do stupid things faster
and with more energy.*

**What do you call a person who
is happy on a Monday?**
Retired.

What does the world's top dentist get?
A little plaque.

**What does a mathematician say
when something goes wrong?**
"Figures!"

**What do you call a psychic who
can't read minds?**
Telepathetic.

**You know what the trouble is
with paperless offices?**
*Everything is great until you
need to use the bathroom.*

Hard work has never killed anyone...
But better not risk it!

Want to hear how I know I was hired for my motivational skills?
Everyone says they have to work twice as hard when I'm around.

What's the best way to make a small fortune on the stock market?
Start off with a big fortune.

How did I lose my job at the bank?
A guy asked me to check his balance, so I pushed him.

What's the definition of a boss?
Someone who is early when you're late and late when you're early.

What happened when the lumberjack couldn't hack it?
They gave him the ax.

Why do retirees count pennies?

They're the only ones who have the time.

How do lawyers say goodbye?

"Sue ya later!"

Did you know there's no official training for trash collectors?

They just pick things up as they go along.

One-Liners

Don't give anyone time to run away with these perfectly timed, gut-busting one-liners.

I ordered a chicken and an egg online,
so I'll let you know.

**I just heard that the person who
invented Velcro died.**
RIP.

I used to believe that all things must pass,
but then I got stuck behind a school bus.

It takes a lot of balls to golf the way I do.

**Correct punctuation is the difference
between a sentence that's well written**
and a sentence that's, well, written.

**My partner just found out I replaced
our bed with a trampoline**
and hit the ceiling.

I decided to sell my vacuum cleaner—
it was just gathering dust.

**Before you criticize someone, you should
walk a mile in their shoes.**
*That way, when you criticize them, you're
a mile away and you have their shoes.*

I saw a sign the other day that said, "Watch for children," and thought,

" That seems like a fair trade."

I went to go buy some camo pants,
but I couldn't find any.

**I got a new pair of gloves the other day,
but they're both "lefts."**
On the one hand, that's actually great.

**So what if I don't know what
"Armageddon" means?**
It's not the end of the world.

**I've spent a lot of time and money
childproofing my house,**
but the kids still get in!

Pollen, or as I like to call it,
*what happens when flowers can't keep
it in their plants.*

Earth's rotation really makes my day.

**I was wondering why the baseball kept
getting bigger and bigger,**
but then it hit me.

Don't you hate it when someone answers their own questions?
I do.

I always say you should take life with a grain of salt.
And a slice of lemon. And a shot of tequila.

Someone gifted me the world's worst thesaurus.
Not only is it awful, it's also awful.

The car looks nice,
but the muffler seems exhausted.

The past, present, and future walked into a bar.
Things got a little tense.

I used to think I was indecisive,
but now I'm not so sure.

You think swimming with dolphins is expensive?
Swimming with sharks costs an arm and a leg.

My kids told me to stop impersonating a flamingo...

... so I had to put my foot down.

**These people have been treating me
like one of the family,**
*and I've put up with it for
as long as I can.*

**Did you know light travels
faster than sound?**
*That's why some people appear bright
before you hear them speak.*

**I threw a boomerang once about
a year ago—**
now I live in constant fear.

Geology rocks,
but geography is where it's at.

**Last night, my friend was complaining
that I never listen to him,**
or something like that.

I was going to tell a time-traveling joke,
but you guys didn't like it.

I like telling Dad jokes.
Sometimes he laughs!

**If I got fifty cents for every
failed math exam,**
I'd have $7.30 by now.

If a parsley farmer is sued,
do they garnish her wages?

**Two fish are in a tank.
One turns to the other and says,**
"Do you know how to drive this thing?"

**The world tongue-twister champion
was just arrested.**
*I hear they're going to give her
a really tough sentence.*

**You'll always stay young if you live well,
eat carefully, sleep enough, play often,**
and lie about your age.

**Today a woman knocked on my door
and asked for a small donation toward
the local swimming pool.**
*I said sure and gave her
a glass of water.*

Shoutout to my fingers—
I can count on all of them.

It was an emotional wedding—
even the cake was in tiers.

My teachers told me I wouldn't amount to much because I'm such a procrastinator.
I told them, "Just you wait!"

You can't believe everything you hear,
but you can repeat it.

I've got a great joke about construction,
but I'm still working on it.

I used to hate facial hair,
but then it grew on me.

I used to be a personal trainer.
Then I gave my too weak notice.

I'll tell you what, it takes guts
to be an organ donor.

Listen, if you're ever attacked by a mob of clowns,
go for the juggler.

I've been told I have a preoccupation for revenge.
We'll see about that.

The last thing I want to do is hurt you,
but it is still on the list.

I'm so good at sleeping,
I can do it with my eyes closed.

I was going to tell you about this elephant I saw on TV,
but then I realized it was irrelephant.

I used to have a handle on life,
but then it broke.

Someone asked me what the difference is between ignorance and apathy.
I told them I don't know and I don't care.

It's easy to make holy water—
you just boil the hell out of it.

I heard there were a bunch of break-ins at the parking garage.
That's wrong on so many levels.

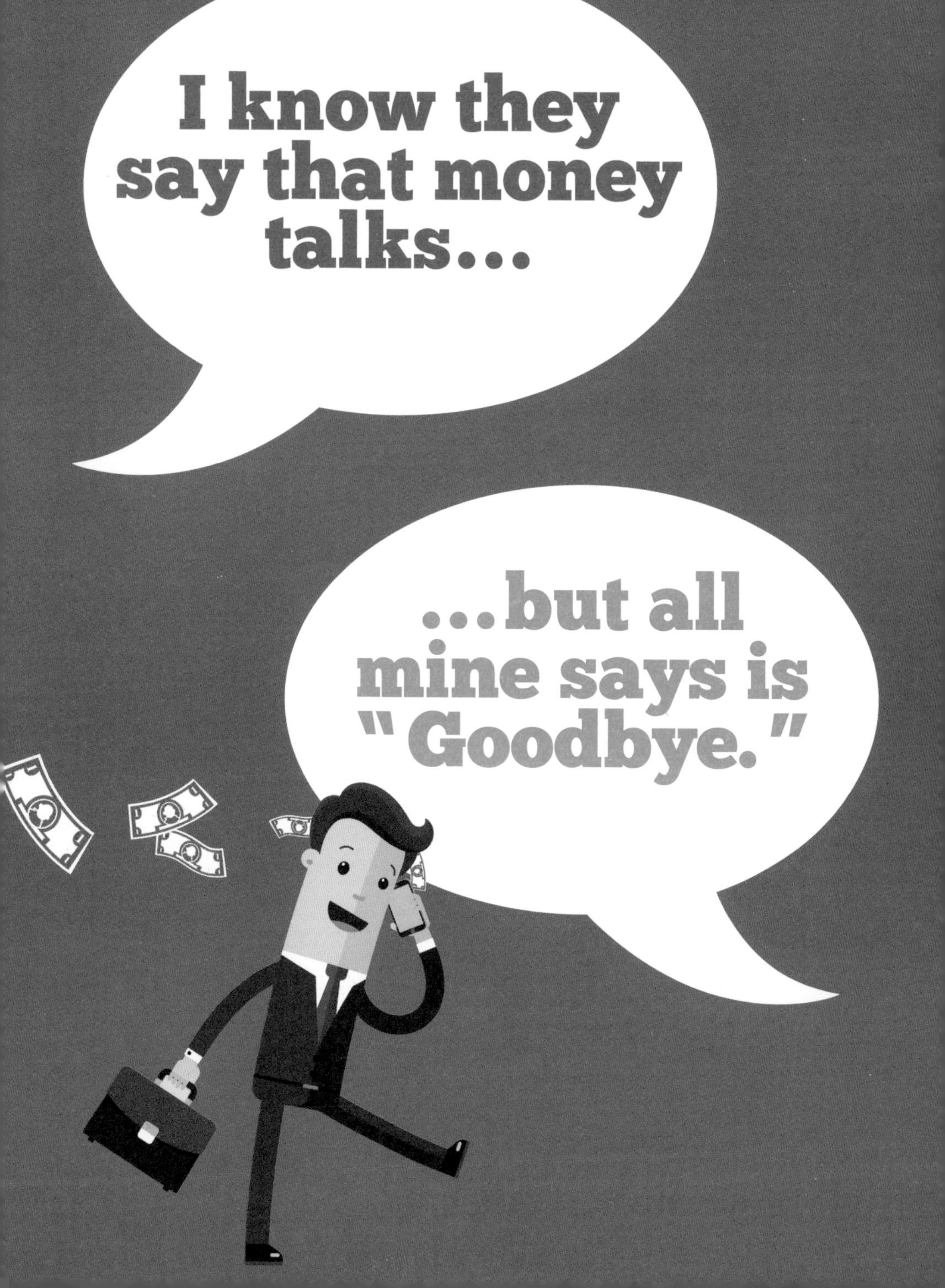
I know they say that money talks...
...but all mine says is "Goodbye."

Russian nesting dolls are so full of themselves.

The person who invented knock-knock jokes should get a no bell prize.

I can't believe I got fired from the calendar factory—
all I did was take the day off!

I didn't think orthopedic shoes would help,
but I stand corrected.

I just got fired from my job as a set designer.
I left without making a scene.

Can I be Frank with you?
I'm thinking of changing my name.

I call refusing to go to the gym a form of resistance training.

Do you think people are born with photographic memories,
or does it take time to develop?

I have a clean conscience.
I've never used it once!

Most people are shocked when they find out how bad I am as an electrician.

The trouble with getting to work on time
is that it makes the day last so long.

Two men walked into a bar.
*You'd think at least one of them
would have ducked.*

People who use selfie sticks really need to take a good, long look at themselves.

The easiest time to add insult to injury is
when you're signing someone's cast.

Avoid cliches like the plague.

**Whenever I tried to use it,
all my Ouija board would tell me
was "Staying Alive."**
*I was concerned until I realized
I was actually using a Bee Gee board.*

Knock-Knock Jokes

Knock, knock! Enjoy the dad joke's most quintessential form with this selection of painfully punny laughs.

Knock, knock
Who's there?
Dishes
Dishes who?
Dishes your father, open up!

Knock, knock
Who's there?
Quiche
Quiche who?
Can I have a hug and a quiche?

Knock, knock
Who's there?
Lena
Lena who?
Lena little closer, and I'll tell
you another joke.

Knock, knock
Who's there?
Wa
Wa who?
What are you so excited about?

Knock, knock
Who's there?
Wooden shoe
Wooden shoe who?
Wooden shoe like to know.

Knock, knock
Who's there?
Wooden shoe
Wooden shoe who?
Wooden shoe like to hear
more jokes?

Knock, knock
Who's there?
Ice cream soda
Ice cream soda who?
Ice cream soda people can hear me!

Knock, knock
Who's there?
Odysseus
Odysseus who?
Odysseus the last straw.

Knock, knock
Who's there?
Cook
Cook who?
There's a chicken in your house??

Knock, knock
Who's there?
Dozen
Dozen who?
Dozen anyone wanna let me in?

Knock, knock
Who's there?
Billy Bob Joe Penny
Billy Bob Joe Penny who?
Really? How many Billy Bob Joe Pennys do you know?

Knock, knock
Who's there?
Cargo
Cargo who?
Cargo beep beep!

Knock, knock
Who's there?
Figs
Figs who?
Figs the doorbell, it's not working!

Knock, knock
Who's there?
Theodore
Theodore who?
Theodore wasn't open so I knocked!

Knock, knock
Who's there?
Haven
Haven who?
Haven you heard enough of these
knock-knock jokes?

Knock, knock
Who's there?
Nobel
Nobel who?
Nobel . . . that's why I knocked!

Knock, knock
Who's there?
Tank.
Tank who?
You're welcome!

Knock, knock
Who's there?
Spell
Spell who?
W-H-O!

Knock, knock
Who's there?
Cash
Cash who?
No thanks, but I'd love some peanuts!

Knock, knock
Who's there?
Armageddon
Armageddon who?
Armageddon a little bored.
Let's get out of here!

Knock, knock
Who's there?
Smellmop
Smellmop who?
Ew, gross!

Knock, knock
Who's there?
Control freak
Contro—
Okay, now you say "control freak who"?

Knock, knock
Who's there?
Keith
Keith who?
Keith me, my thweet prince!

Knock, knock
Who's there?
Europe
Europe who?
No, you're a poo!

Knock, knock
Who's there?
Owls say
Owls say who?
That's correct.

Knock, knock
Who's there?
To
To who?
Actually, it's "to whom."

Knock, knock
Who's there?
Beats
Beats who?
Beats me!

Knock, knock
Who's there?
Ida
Ida who?
I think it's pronounced Idaho.

Knock, knock
Who's there?
Kent
Kent who?
Kent you tell by the sound of my voice?

Knock, knock
Who's there?
Radio
Radio who?
Radio not, here I come!

Knock, knock
Who's there?
Reed
Reed who?
Redo? Alright. Knock, knock

Knock, knock
Who's there?
Ears
Ears who?
Ears another knock-knock joke!

Knock, knock
Who's there?
Dejah
Dejah who?
Knock, knock

Knock, knock
Who's there?
I am
I am who?
I don't know, you tell me.

Knock, knock
Who's there?
Candice
Candice who?
Candice joke get any worse?

Knock, knock
Who's there?
Honeydew
Honeydew who?
Honeydew you mind getting
the door?

Knock, knock

Who's there?

Alpaca

Alpaca who?

Alpaca bag, you pack a suitcase!

Knock, knock
Who's there?
Major
Major who?
Major day with this joke, haven't I?

Knock, knock
Who's there?
FBI
FBI wh—
We're asking the questions here.

Knock, knock
Who's there?
Ho-ho
Ho-ho who?
Your Santa impression needs work.

Knock, knock
Who's there?
Justin
Justin who?
Justin the neighborhood—
thought I'd drop by.

Knock, knock
Who's there?
Gorilla
Gorilla who?
Gorilla burger, I brought buns!

Knock, knock
Who's there?
Boo
Boo who?
Don't cry, it's just a joke.

Knock, knock
Who's there?
Etch
Etch who?
Gesundheit!

Knock, knock
Who's there?
Dewey
Dewey who?
Dewey have to do this
every time?

Knock, knock
Who's there?
Ray
Ray who?
Ray-member me? It's your dad.

Knock, knock
Who's there?
Russell
Russell who?
Russell up some food, I'm starving.

Knock, knock
Who's there?
Broken pencil
Broken pencil who?
Never mind, there's no point.

Knock, knock
Who's there?
Dozen
Dozen who?
Dozen all this knocking
bother you?

Knock, knock
Who's there?
Orange
Orange who?
Orange you sick of these knock-knock jokes yet?

Knock, knock
Who's there?
Says
Says who?
Says me, that's who!

Knock, knock
Who's there?
Vladislav
Vladislav who?
Vladislav. Baby don't hurt me.
Don't hurt me no more.

Family

Some call it chaos, you call
it parenting. When things
are truly dire, bring out these
jokes for a laugh if you
just can't cry any longer.

**What's the difference between a
good parent and a great one?**

*Good parents let you lick the beaters.
Great parents turn them off first.*

Why is a computer so smart?

It listens to its motherboard.

Do dads always snore?

No. Only when they're sleeping.

**After nearly fifty years, my grandmother has
finally gotten my grandfather to stop biting
his nails. Do you want to know how?**

She hid his teeth.

**My grandfather started walking five
miles a day when he turned sixty.**

*He's eighty now, and we have
no idea where he is.*

**What do you call your mom's angry
French sister?**

A crossaunt.

What is parenting?

Missing your kids when they're asleep and missing your sanity when they're awake.

What did the drummer call his twin daughters?

Anna one, Anna two.

When does a joke become a dad joke?

When it becomes apparent.

What do tomatoes say to their kids when they're falling behind on a walk?

"You need to ketchup!"

What do you need to master before becoming a parent?

The art of the one-minute poop and the half-minute shower.

How do you teach kids about taxes?

Eat a third of their sandwich.

How do you put a baby alien to sleep?

You rocket.

What's the definition of karma?

When your kids turn out exactly like you.

**What did the snowman put
over its baby's crib?**

A snowmobile.

**How can you tell the difference between
children and teenagers?**

*Children gain knowledge by asking
lots of questions, and teenagers
already know everything.*

**What did the father cow say
to the baby cow?**

"It's pasture bedtime."

**Why do teenagers travel in
odd-numbered groups?**

Because they can't even.

**What did the daddy ghost say
to the baby ghost?**

"Fasten your sheet belt."

**What are the most popular perfumes
for ages twelve to eighteen?**

Adolescents.

What did the baby corn say to the mom corn?

"Where's popcorn?"

**Did you hear about the kidnapping
on the bus?**

It's fine! He woke up.

What do preteen ducks hate?

When their voice quacks.

What fruits do twins love?

Pears.

**What do you call a childless person
telling dad jokes?**

A faux pa.

Why did the baby broom go to bed?

It was very sweepy.

**What's the difference between
a badly dressed kid on a bicycle and
a well-dressed kid on a tricycle?**

Attire.

What did the buffalo say when his son left?

"Bison!"

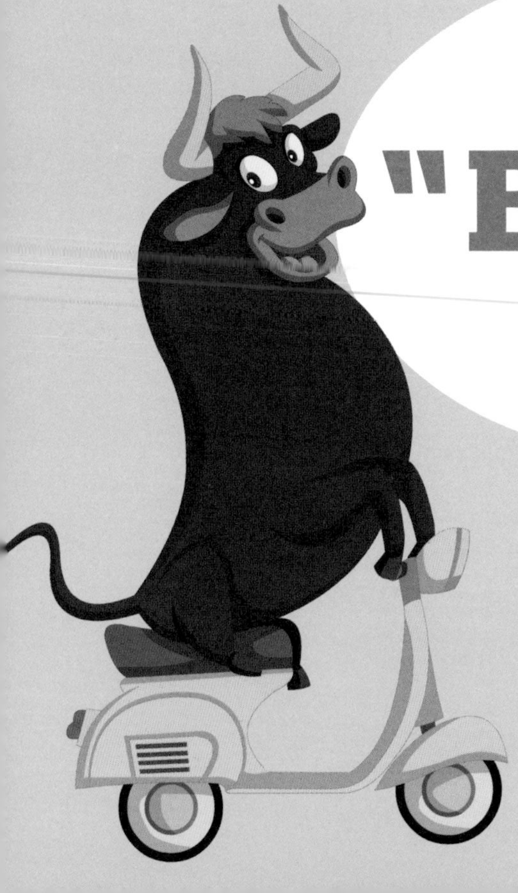

Why do dads take an extra pair of socks when they go golfing?

In case they get a hole in one.

Where do baby cats learn to swim?

The kitty pool.

How is being a dad like shaving?

No matter how good a job you do, you always have to do it again the next day.

What do you call your dad if he falls through ice?

A Popsicle.

How is a baby bird like her dad?

She's a chirp off the old block.

What did the mama color wheel say to the baby color wheel?

"Don't use that tone with me!"

Where do baby apes sleep?

In apricots.

What's the best way to raise a baby dinosaur?

With a crane.

**What makes more noise than
a toddler?**

Two toddlers.

**What makes more noise than
two toddlers?**

A teenager slamming their door.

**Why did the baby put quarters
in its diaper?**

It needed to be changed.

**Why did the kid cross the
playground?**

To get to the other slide.

What do snowmen call their kids?

Chill-dren.

**What branch of the military
accepts toddlers?**

The infantry.

**I was horrified when I found out my
six-year-old child wasn't mine.**

*I really need to pay more attention
during school pick-up.*

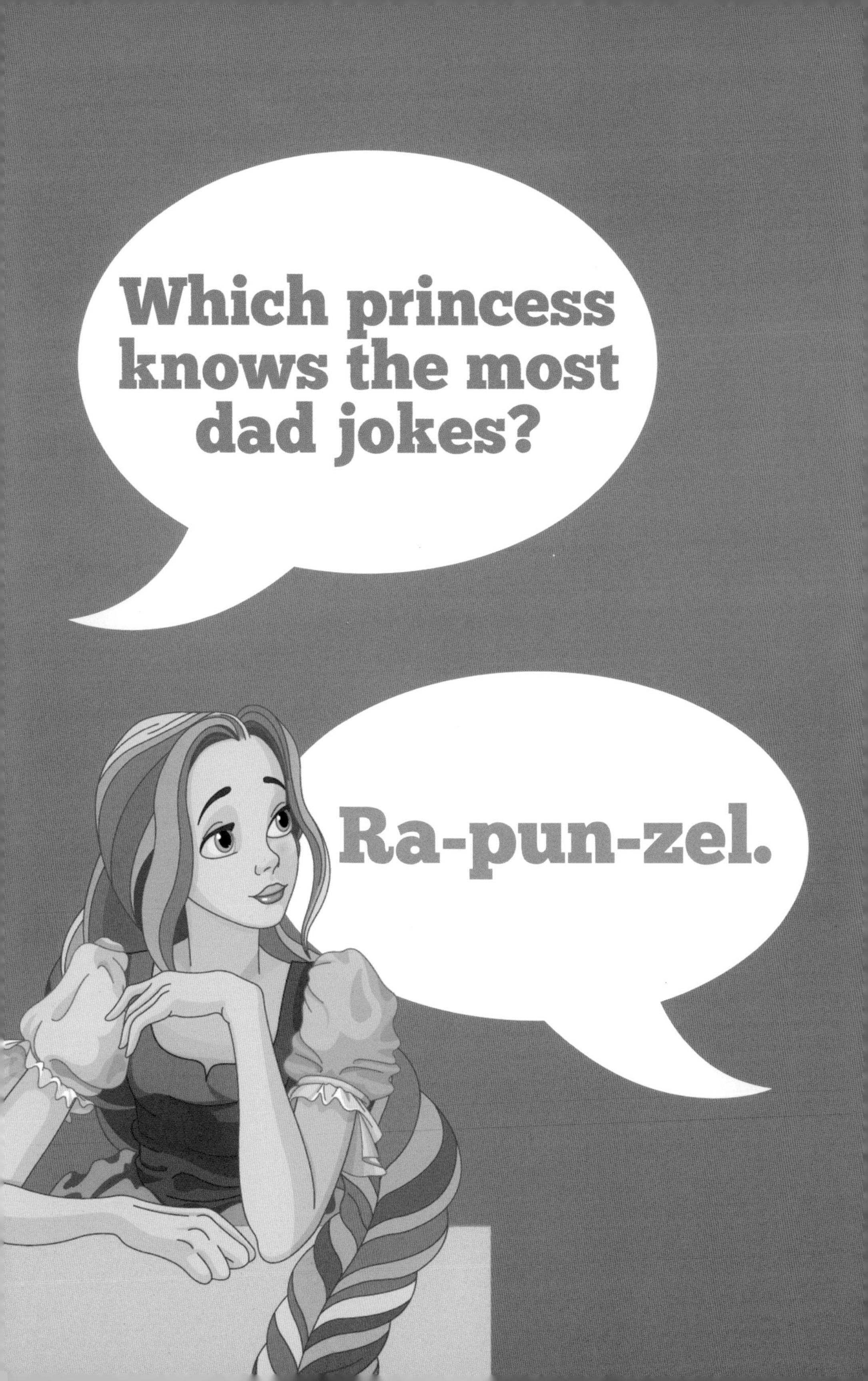
Which princess knows the most dad jokes?
Ra-pun-zel.

A woman in labor suddenly shouted, "Shouldn't! Wouldn't! Couldn't! Didn't!"
"Don't worry," said the doctor. "Those are just contractions."

I got my son a fridge for his birthday.
I can't wait to see his face light up when he opens it.

What do potatoes call their children?
Tater tots.

What do you call a kangaroo's lazy baby?
A pouch potato.

Fine Dining

Laughs perfect for any dining occasion. Test some of these jokes on the waiter—your family will *love* it.

How do you keep a bagel from getting away?
You put lox on it.

What did the shark say when he ate the clownfish?
"This tastes a little funny."

A bear went out to dinner and said, "I'll have the salmon . . . and a soda." The waiter asked, "What's with the pause?"
The bear replied, "I was born with them."

What's orange and sounds like a carrot?
A parrot.

Once my dog ate all the Scrabble tiles.
He kept leaving messages around the house.

Why did the Oreo go to the dentist?
It lost its filling.

What do cornflakes wear on their feet?
Kelloggs.

**What do you get from a
pampered cow?**

Spoiled milk.

**What happens when you pour
root beer in a square glass?**

You just have beer.

**What's the best food to eat when you're
so hungry you could eat a house?**

*Cottage cheese, wall nuts,
and kitchen sink cookies.*

**What do you call a rooster staring
at a pile of lettuce?**

A chicken sees a salad.

**What do you call a locomotive full
of bubblegum?**

A chew–chew train.

**What do you call a bear
with no teeth?**

A gummy bear.

**What's the best way to embarrass
a vegetable?**

You roast it.

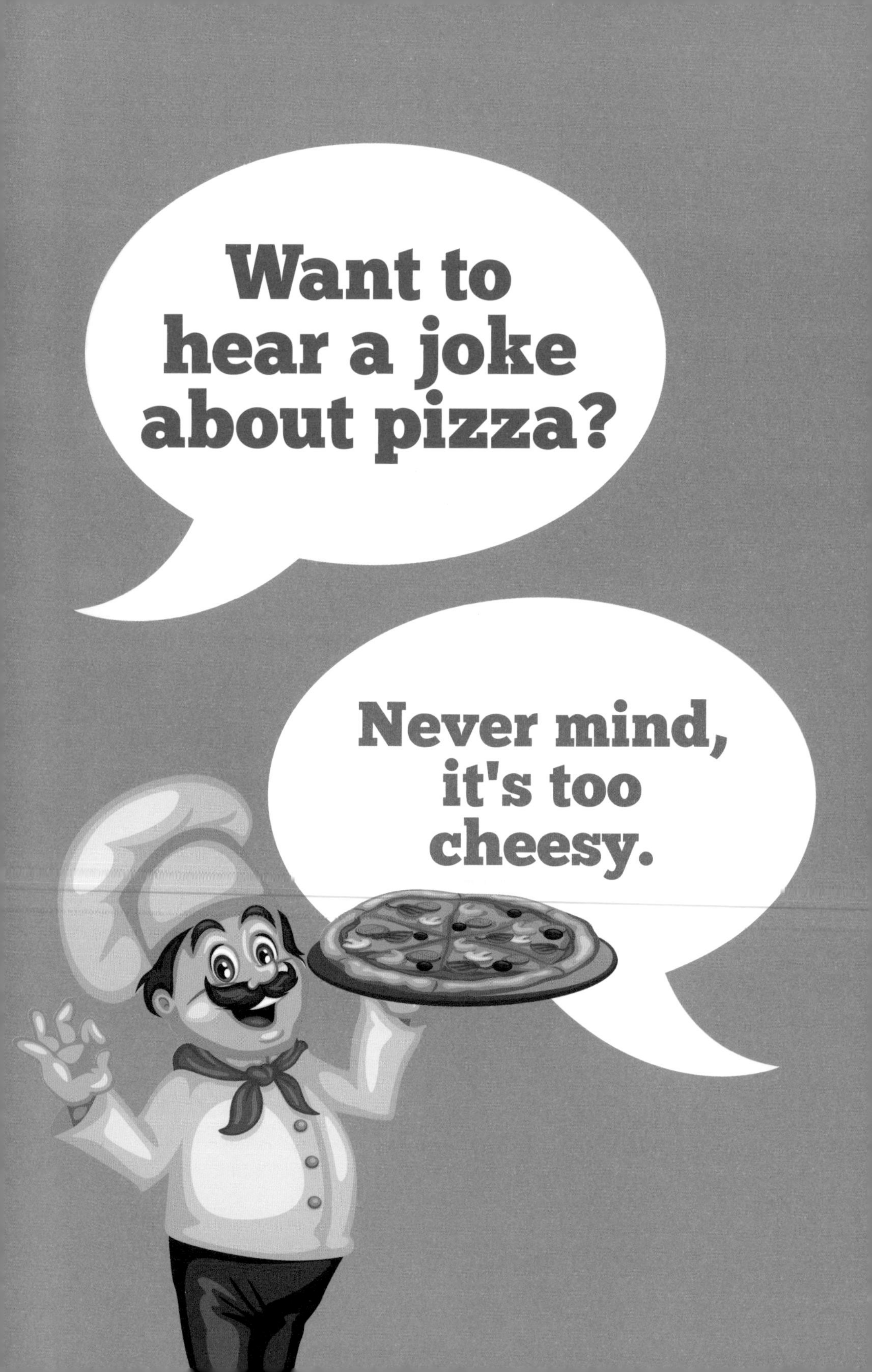
Want to hear a joke about pizza?
Never mind, it's too cheesy.

Why do melons have big weddings?
They cantaloupe.

What did the mayonnaise say when the fridge door opened?
"Hang on a minute! I'm dressing."

What's the main ingredient in canned laughter?
Processed cheese.

How do you make an apple turnover?
Push it downhill.

Where did the broccoli go to have a few drinks?
The salad bar.

Why are butchers so funny?
They're always hamming it up.

Why shouldn't you tell a secret on a farm?
Because the potatoes have eyes and the corn has ears.

Why was the carrot such a great detective?
It could get to the root of every case.

**What did the grape say when
it was squished?**
Nothing, it just let out a little wine.

**Why did the orange stop rolling
down the hill?**
It ran out of juice.

**Why didn't the sesame seed want
to leave the casino?**
It was on a roll.

**How do you measure the weight
of crackers?**
In grahams.

**How can you tell if there's an elephant
in your refrigerator?**
You can't close it.

**What do you call a group of
strawberries playing guitar?**
A jam session.

When does coffee taste like dirt?

When it's ground.

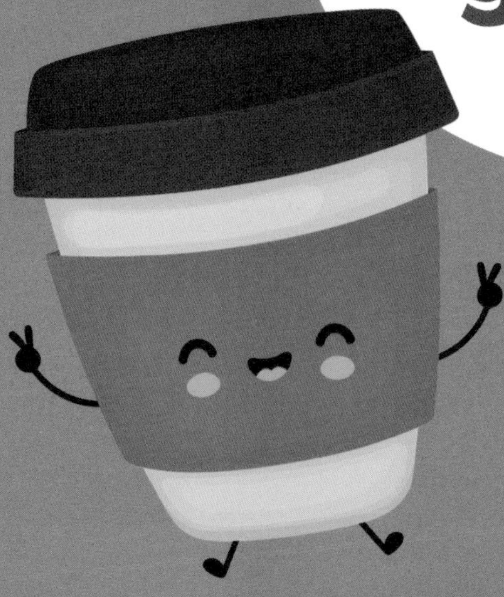

What do you call a fake noodle?
An impasta.

**What did the egg say to the mixer
after an argument?**
"I know when I'm beaten."

**What's the easiest way to make
a banana split?**
Cut it in half.

**What do you call a sheep that works
at a fried-food stand?**
A battering ram.

Where does bread rise?
In the yeast.

**What do you call a shoe made
from a banana?**
A slipper.

**How can you tell the difference between
an orange and a walrus?**
*Give it a squeeze. If you don't get
orange juice, it's a walrus.*

**What do you call the king
of vegetables?**
Elvis Parsley.

How do chickens bake a cake?
From scratch.

**What does a clock do after
dinner?**
It goes back for seconds.

What vegetables do sailors hate?
Leeks.

How do you turn soup into gold?
You add fourteen carrots.

Vegetable puns make me feel good.
No, really! From my head tomatoes.

Someone told me that all apples are yellow.
I told her, "That's bananas."

**Did you hear the rumor about
peanut butter?**
Well, I'm not going to spread it.

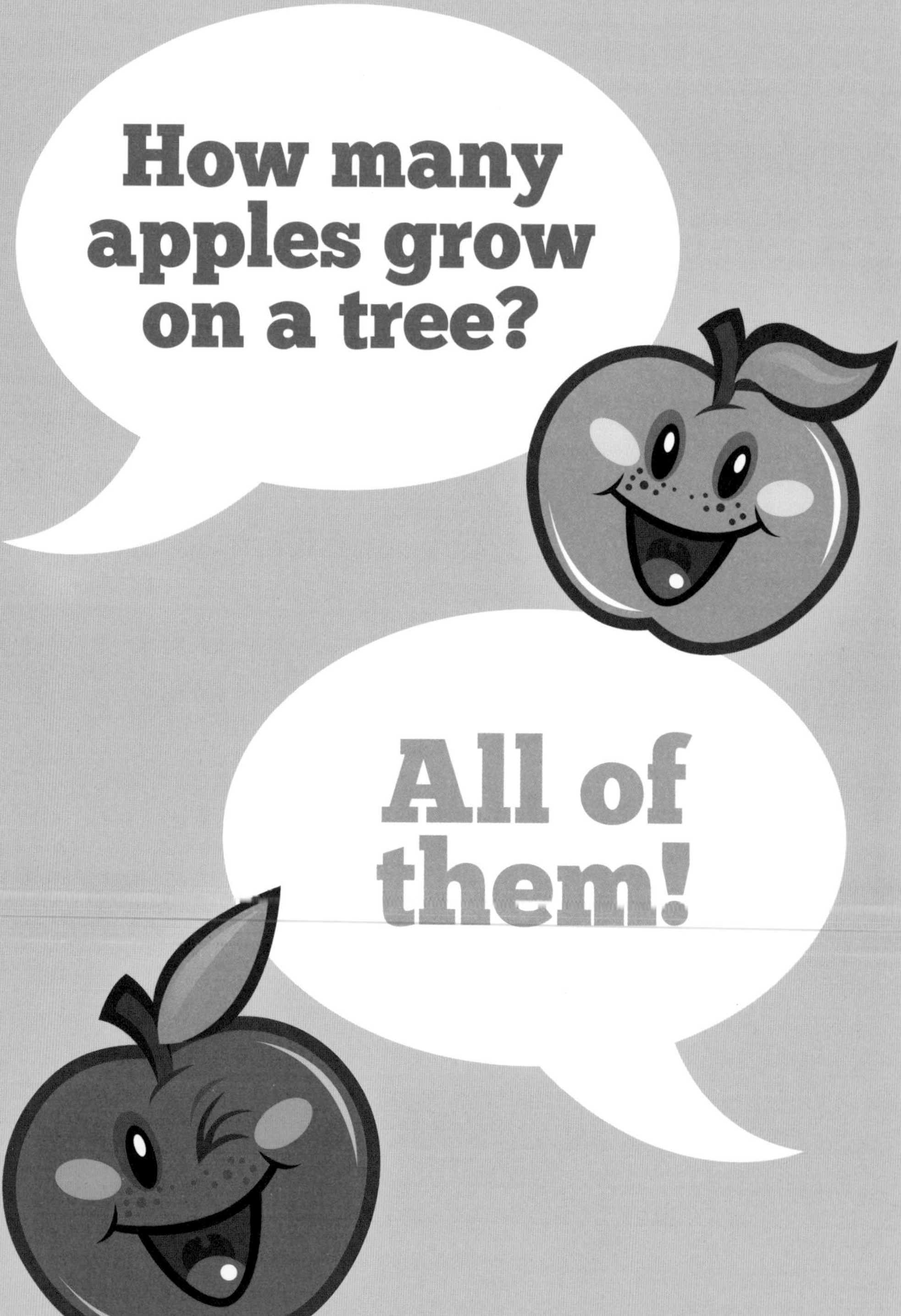
How many apples grow on a tree?
All of them!

**My spaghetti got into the
Book of World Records.**
*I just hope I can clean
the pages.*

Did you hear about the salad race?
*The lettuce was ahead and the
tomato tried to ketchup.*

Why shouldn't you tease egg whites?
They can't take a yolk.

What cheese is made backwards?
Edam.

Why did the T. rex eat raw meat?
Its arms couldn't reach the oven.

**Which vegetables go best with
jacket potatoes?**
Button mushrooms.

Why did the fisherman order fish for dinner?
Just for the halibut.

Highbrow Humor

You're as deep as they get, so tell some jokes that will inspire great minds. Just don't stick around for any follow-up questions.

**Why are Russian playwrights
so organized?**

*They like to Chekhov things on
their to-do lists.*

**What should you do when painting
a portrait of Lucifer?**

Be sure to give the devil his hue.

**My friend had never read
Jane Austen.**

However, she was open to Persuasion.

**What do you need to write about
time travel?**

The ability to think outside the clock.

How do Impressionist painters get around?

Degas makes de Van Gogh.

**What do you call a citrus fruit that
grows underwater?**

Sublime.

**Did you hear about the poet who wrote
about digging holes?**

He was very deep.

How was Shakespeare able to write so many plays?
He had some serious quill power.

What do you call a reptile who likes to pick a fight?

An instigator.

What does it mean if your friend from Prague is wearing a suit of armor?

The Czech is in the mail.

Why did Louis XIV have trouble designing Versailles?

He was too baroque.

Argon, helium, and xenon walk into a bar. The bartender shouts "We don't serve noble gases here!"

The gases do not react.

Why did the Archaeopteryx always get the worm?

Because it was an early bird.

Did you hear about the woman who got a PhD in palindromes?

Her name is Dr. Awkward.

How do Vikings send messages?

They use Norse code.

What do you call it when you hire actors to play spies?

Thespionage.

I went to the library and asked for a book about Pavlov and Schrödinger.

The librarian said, "It rings a bell, but I don't know if it's there or not."

Descartes walks into a bar and the bartender asks if he wants to try the house special.

He says, "I think not!" and disappears.

Why would Elizabethan poets make terrible rappers?

They're all dead.

What number is the dirtiest to say in public?

288. It's two gross.

Where do library-goers most often slip and fall?

In the Non-Friction section.

Why did the book go to the hospital?

To get its appendix removed.

Who designed the Round Table for King Arthur?
Sir Cumference.

What is Beowulf's favorite snack?

Hwæt thins.

What dinosaur wrote the best romance novels?

The Brontësaurus.

Did I tell you someone stole my dictionary?

Now I'm lost for words.

How do you know if your spouse is dreaming about hobbits?

They're Tolkien in their sleep.

What's the difference between a cat and a comma?

One has claws at the end of its paws, and the other's a pause at the end of a clause.

What made "Civil Disobedience" such a great essay?

Thoreau editing.

Why was the shadow puppet theater less financially successful than expected?

Those were just projected figures.

How do you get a musician off your porch?

Give them twenty bucks and take the pizza.

Middle C, E flat, and G walk into a bar.

"Sorry," says the bartender, "we don't serve minors."

What was Beethoven's favorite fruit?

Ba-na-na-naaa.

What's Shakespeare's favorite video game character?

Sonnet the Hedgehog.

A dad walks into a bookstore and asks for a play by Shakespeare. The clerk asks, "Which one?"

The dad says, "William."

What do you call a surrealist musical?

Hello, Dali!

What do you call it when plays get messy in the second act?

Chekhov's gunk.

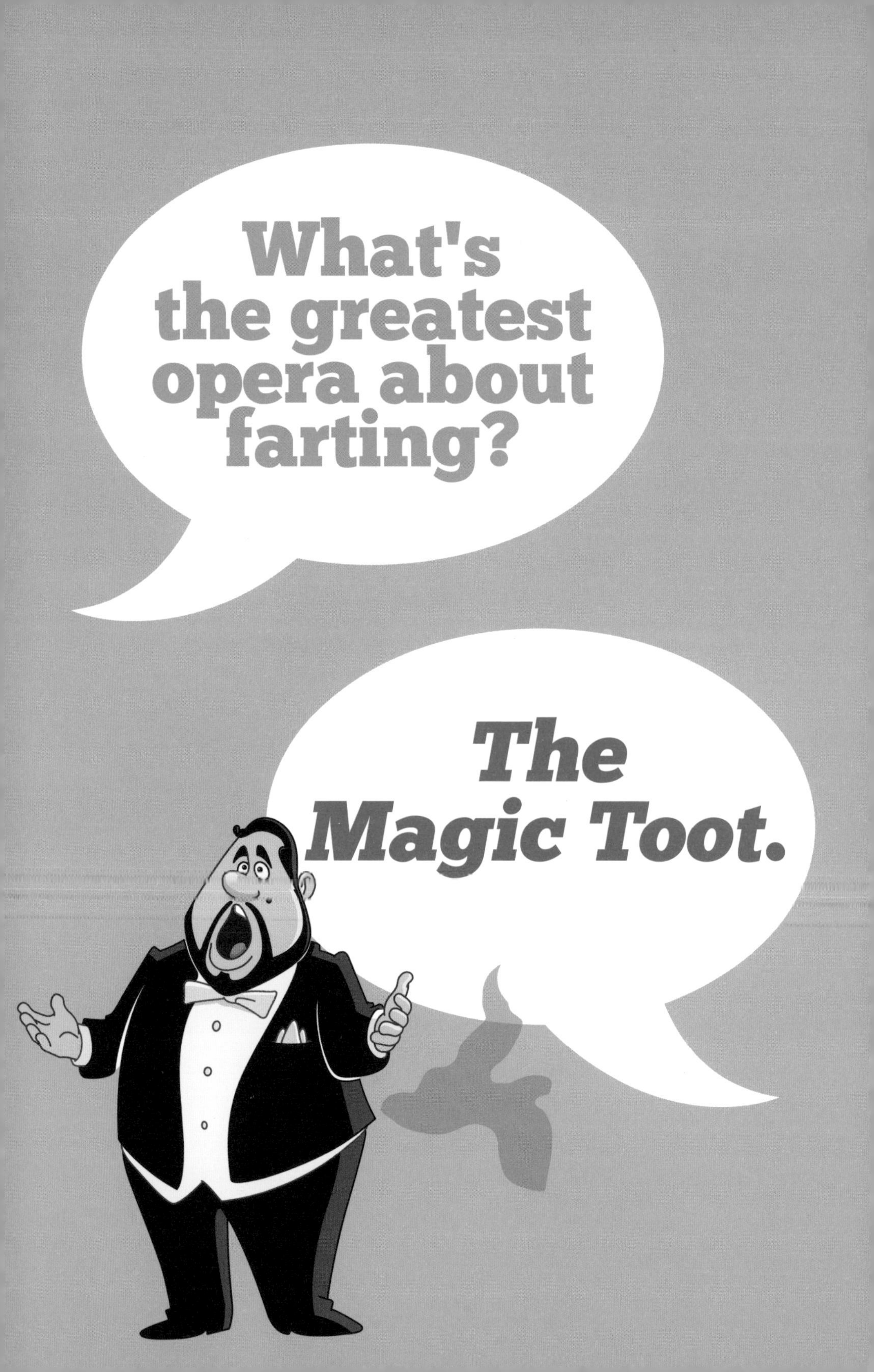
What's the greatest opera about farting?
The Magic Toot.

**What do poets use to call
their girlfriends?**

A Sapphone.

**Where did the Greek messenger god
shop for tools and appliances?**

Herm Depot.

What do you call a fake epic poem?

A Fraudyssey.

**What do you call an epic poem
about a barbecue?**

The Grilliad.

**What do you call an even older
epic poem about a barbecue?**

The Epic of Grillgamesh.

**What do you call Greek heroes
who run out of gasoline?**

Car-go-nots.

**What Greek mythical figure was
Instagram famous?**

Social Medea.

**Why did Pythagoras wind up with
two dates for the prom?**

He was in a love triangle.

**Which Shakespearean characters
give famous speeches about
lunch meat?**

Hamlet and Baloneyus.

What do you call a goth composer?

Bach in black.

**What do you say to a Greek tragedian
who tore your jeans?**

Euripides!

Why did J. S. Bach have twenty kids?

Because his organ had no stops.

Why is baroque music better in winter?

Because in summer it's too hot to Handel.

**When is it hardest to find a
classical composer?**

When he's Haydn.

What do Alexander the Great and Winnie the Pooh have in common?

They have the same middle name.

What's the opposite of irony?

Wrinkly.

Where did Caesar keep his armies?

Up his sleevies.

What's the best thing about Switzerland?

I'm not sure, but their flag is a huge plus.

And God said to John, "Come forth and you shall be granted eternal life."

But then John came in fifth and won a toaster.

Helvetica and Times New Roman walk into a bar.

"Get out of here!" shouts the bartender. "We don't serve your type."

How does Moses make his tea?

Hebrews it.

**What does Charles Dickens keep
in his spice rack?**

*The best of thymes, and the
worst of thymes.*

**Why did the yogurt go to
the art museum?**

Because it was cultured.

**What do you call an apology written
in dots and dashes?**

Re-morse code.

How do poets say hello?

"Hey, haven't we metaphor?"

**The numbers 19 and 20 got
into a fight.**

21.

Ultimate Comebacks

Catch them by surprise!
Here's what to say when
your kid says...

Did you get a haircut?
No, I got them all cut.

How do I look?
With your eyes.

Can you make me a sandwich?
Poof! You're a sandwich.

Can you put my shoes on?
I don't think they'll fit me.

I'm cold.
Then sit in the corner—it's 90 degrees.

**I'm having trouble with these
math problems.**
*Tell math to grow up and solve
its own problems.*

Can you put the dog out?
I didn't know it was on fire.

Do you want a box for your leftovers?
No, but I'll wrestle you for them.

So?
No, but I knit a little.

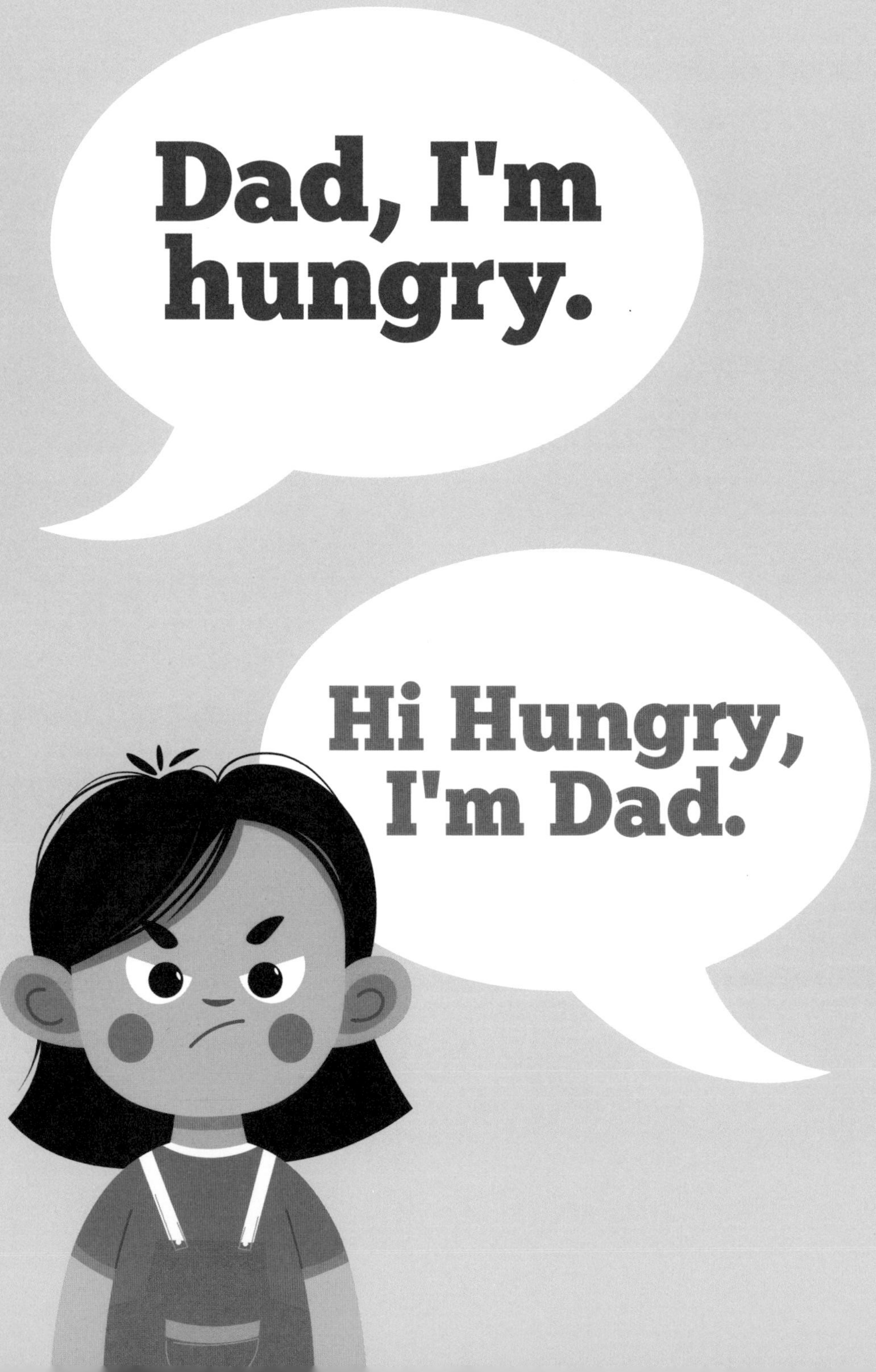
Dad, I'm hungry.
Hi Hungry, I'm Dad.

How do you feel?
With my hands.
What about you?

What's up?
It's a kids' movie.

Nice beard.
Thanks, it's growing on me.

Will you be around?
If I'm not being a square.

What time is it?
Time to get a watch.

How's the water?
Wet.

Can I have a hand?
Sure. (Start clapping.)

I feel like takeout tonight.

Weird, you don't look like takeout.

What's up?

(Look up at the ceiling.) I don't see anything.

I feel like garbage.

Really? I'm in the mood for pizza.

Do you want seafood?

I'd prefer to eat it.

Can you play piano by ear?

No, but I can use my hands.

Don't pick your nose!

I didn't pick it! I was born with it.

Do you want to eat sushi?

I don't know, it's a little fishy!

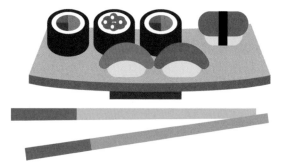

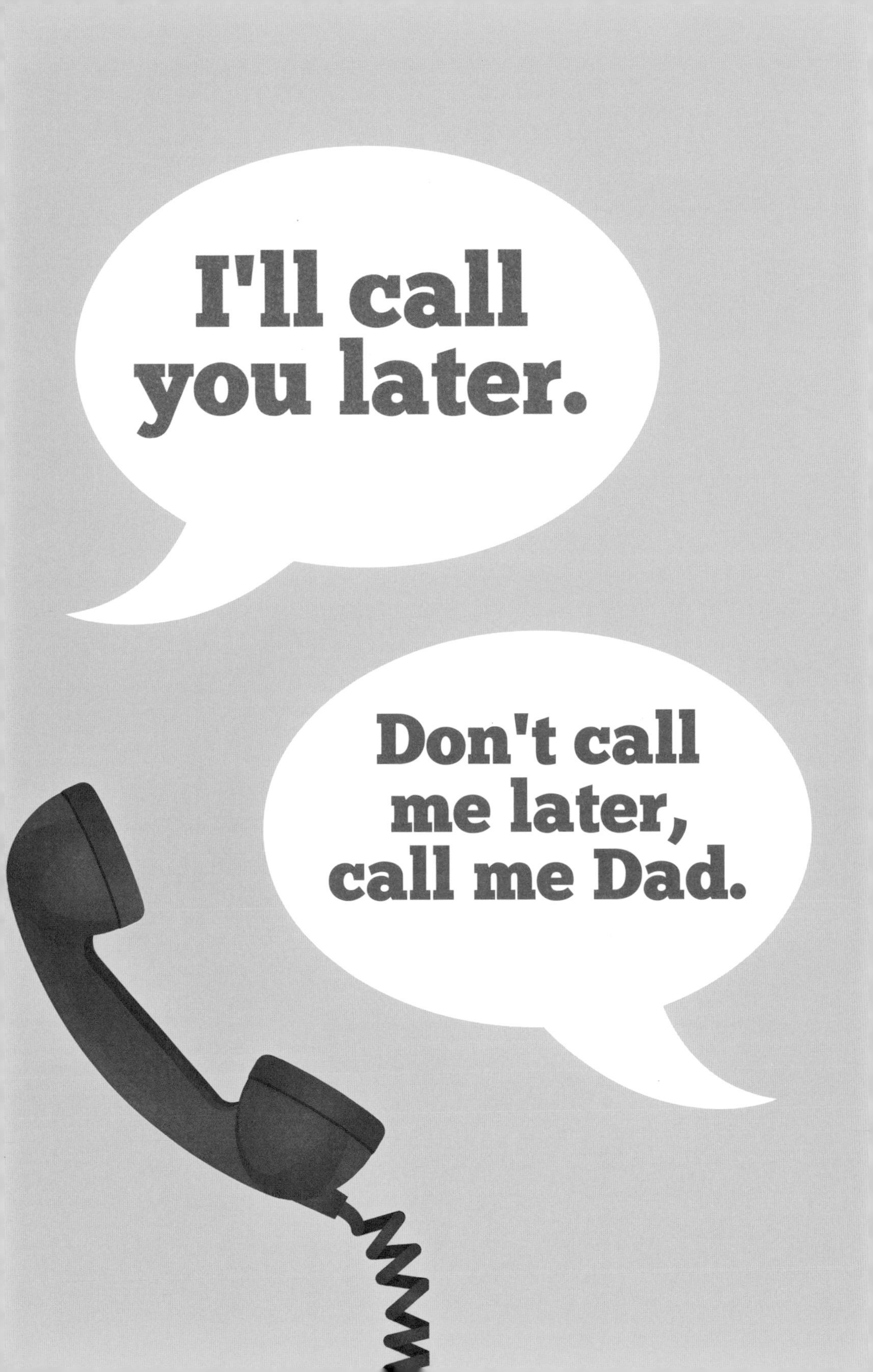
I'll call you later.
Don't call me later, call me Dad.

How are you?
My lawyer says I don't have to answer that question.

**The early bird gets
the worm.**
*If the early bird gets the worm,
I'll sleep in until there's pancakes.*

Dad, I'm serious.
Since when is your name "Serious"?

What's the movie about?
It's about two hours.

Can I watch TV?
Sure, as long as you don't turn it on.

Can my friend sleep over?
*Does your friend usually
sleep under?*

Can I have a bookmark?
*I've been your father this long and
you still think my name is Mark?*

How was your day?
Too early to say, it hasn't finished yet.

Dear Dad,

....

....

....

....

....

....

....

....

....

....

....

Love, Me